For Marlene and Daniel —
my two dear friends —
and with appreciation to Daniel
especially for the work we have
done together — Love —
Kit

A FOUR GATHERING

CAPRA PRESS   SANTA BARBARA   1981

LIBRARY OF CONGRESS CATALOGING IN PUBLICATION DATA

Main entry under title:

A Four gathering.

　　1. American poetry—California—Santa
Barbara.　2. American poetry—Women authors.
3. American poetry—20th century.　I. Peake,
Katy.
PS572.S35F6　　　811'.54'0809287　　　81-18030
ISBN 0-88496-178-8　　　　　　　　AACR2
ISBN 0-88496-177-X　(pbk.)

CAPRA PRESS
Post Office Box 2068
Santa Barbara, California 93120

TABLE OF CONTENTS

Katy Peake

PLATT RIVER HOLDOUT

Where last month tassled ranks of corn linked
farm to farm across the prairie miles,
now each is solitaire, an island of abandoned totems,
squatting in the grit and silt of river leavings.

Here rib-sprung silos totter, stinking of fermented grain
in clouds of drunk and dying flies, above the sagging
roofs of barns and sheds where discs and harrows rust with
algae in their teeth and cows drowned in their stanchions.

Here hot winds fret the buried fields and pock the panes
of empty drift-flanked houses, spraddled derelict over
vine-stripped porches, like mired beasts listening
to the ceaseless night bird cries of dry windmills.

Here too a man plows, inscribing the legend of fifty years'
domain, the unmarked boundaries of his lost holdings so
fixed, he does not pause to note the turns or shift his head
to watch the crumbling furrows fill with dust behind him.

HUNTER'S WIFE

They enter boldly and shed the night
with sage sweet jackets brightly plaid
and steaming boots.
The black dog wags to general praise
reserving eyes for one
A final shower from his rain-soaked coat
he settles down before the fire
to lick his muddy paws
Guns made safe lean muzzle up
Game bags yield for a kitchen count
before the drinks are served
The only woman John says proudly
who doesn't mind the dirty work
I will not tell him that I cannot wait
until the broken birds are naked
and the bright wings out of sight.

IN CAMERA

Like an object stared at and transposed
To the red cave of the inner lid
I see my mother's face, a negative,
Exchanging light for dark
Not a memory but a presence
Appearing on its own terms
The instant before waking

NIGHTWATCH

Just before dusk
The great horned owl gliding
Cloud silent across the lawn
Lofting to a high dead branch
Among the Scottish pines

Muffling winds about him
Like a wizard's cloak he turns
His tufted head from side to side
Gathering the failing light
Into his golden eyes

Above a garden struck
To sudden fearful stillness
This artful night lord waits
With ears attuned for dark to claim
The memory of his shadow

At dawn his perch is bare
Beneath it neatly packaged
Feathers fur and bone
My tame grey squirrel is missing
From a garden full of song

RONDA DE NOCHE

Entre dos luces viene
el gran buho de cuerno
aplaneando en silencio de nubes
al través de la hierba
levantándose por arriba
hasta una rama desecada
del pino escosés

Arropándose las alas
como capo de brujo
se revuelve la cabeza penuchada
de lado a lado
recogiendo dentro los ojos aúreos
la última luz

Sobre el jardín
de repente agarrado
por una calma temerosa
este sabio señor de la noche acecha
hasta que trague la obscuridad
la memoria de su sombra

Al alba se encuentra
desamparada la perca
por abajo paquitos aseados
de plumas, pelo, y huesos
Al jardín lleno de reclamos
falta mi ardillita amansada

HOMECOMING

Along the lane
rain levelled wagon ruts
and yours the first shoes
to blot a season's fretwork
of skunk, racoon and bird tracks.

Rows of unpruned pears and cherry-plums
split limbs drooping
over circles of fallen fruit.
Clustered wasps at suck
gorging on the rotting pulp.

The front gate dragging on its broken hinge
mocks the rasp of crickets
breeding in the walls and floorboards
of these godforsaken rooms.

The hearthstones burried
in the dust and scattered ashes
of long dead fires.
Everywhere — the stink of mice

Answers to letters you never wrote.

REGRESANDO

Por la vereda
carriles allanados por lluvia
y los zapatos tuyos
los primeros que borran
huellas de mofetas, mapaches, y pájaros
calados de la estación.

Filas de perales y cerezos
la escamonda descuidada
ramas resquebradas, pendiendo
sobre círculos de frutas caídas.
Avispas apiñadas chupando
saciándose de la pulpa podrida.

El portillo arrastando del gozne quebrado
imita a raspear de grillos   .
procreando en paredes y tablados
de estos cuartos desamparados.

La chimenea enterrada en polvo y cenizas
derramadas de fuegos
hace mucho tiempo muertos.
En todas partes — hedor de ratones

Respuestas a cartas que nunca has escrito.

LANDSCAPE PAINTING

I think she must have left the train between stations
and stood watching unnoticed as it pulled away,
rolling up its track behind it like a carpet,
leaving the ground unmarked.
I see her calmly setting up her easel, beginning to paint.
Perhaps ravens feed her or she feels no need of food,
too engrossed filling her canvas with small grey strokes,
like feathers laid one by one on the breast of a dove.
They become a landscape in which earth and sky meet
In clouds or mountains. Without horizon.
The light, a shadowless diffusion, any time of day.
Points of the compass unhinted. In the middle distance
there are figures which may be flying or floating.
They do not touch. No embraces. No blows.
In blind faces only mouths are open, silently screaming.
Beside the painting is a white card which says:
"My Place in Life" by Elinor S. Not for sale.

NIGHT MOTHER, DARKEN MY GYPSY'S WAY

Night Mother, darken my gypsy's way.
Tangle his flight with cloud.
Over the rack of this mountain's back
stretch a shadow net to shroud
clefts and gullies that edge the track,
and let no errant moonlight stray
to keep his stumbling feet from stones.
Fill his wandering heart with fears.
Let him find your streams in flood
and know the salted sting of tears.
Until they tame his gypsy blood
send your winds to chill his bones.
Let him tremble at your wrath
and beg of you to stay his fate.
Let him curse his fall from grace
Til cock tells owl he's up too late.
Then when he prays to see my face
Dawn Mother, brighten my gypsy's path.

LET US NOW PRAISE FAMOUS MEN

Singly or in pairs
they buy him drinks
and linger briefly
at his corner table
smiling at his inappropriate
laughter and spittled beard
while their eyes dart
like weasles looking for cover
among understanding friends.
The great bell-toned voice is cracked,
thick tongued, a wooden clapper
washed in fool's gold of malt whiskey
and phlegm of drowning lungs.
The thread of wit lost
to the minotaur within,
he wanders that dimming cavern
toward the day when
cheerful in black suits
they will mourn the great days
of his leadership.

WHILE LYING BENEATH A FAVORITE TREE

If what I can see from here
is all that I will ever see
I would find these branches eloquent
with the shapes of spiders, dolphins, tigers and man
strong and weak in their season
large or small according to the mind's scale
These clouds will be mountains
heaving through the earth's crust
or the lost city of Atlantis
And that unlimited inner eye
would find itself at home in the chambers of moles
sharing the journey of seedlings
Everything I have known or can imagine
I would tell to the passing planets
until my story is told
and even memory is content to sleep

OLD DOG

It's a boney packet my old dog makes
in his coat as scruff as summer stubble
over a rack of washboard ribs.
His elbows, knobs of elephant grey.

    I see him

scuff on shabby slipper feet
into a patch of winter sun and sigh.
Folding his aches and pains together, he wraps
them with a tail as beaded as a rosary

    and tells his years.

Kit Tremaine

HAWK

sharp-eyed death flies low
on this winter day
and from the deerpath
I feel his passing
in the rush of air

soft, sibilant is the sound

and in one breath I sense
that I am death
I fly between his wings
the same cold wind that bears him up
tears sharply at my face

the same cold chill knifes through my bones

the hawk's harsh need
has now become my own
and I too hunt the meadow

HALCÓN

Muerte, penetrante de ojo,
vuela bajo
este día del invierno
y en la senda del ciervo
siento su vuelo
en la prisa del aíre

tierno, sibilante el sonido

en un aliento
sé . . . soy la Muerte,
vuelo entre sus alas
y rompiendo mi cara
el mismo viento frío
que le lleva en cielo

acuchillando por mis huesos
el mismo escalofrío fuerte

la necesidad dura del Halcón
ahora es la mía
y también cazo la pradera . . . . .

DEATH OF MY FATHER...MY SELF

a skeleton, a bag of skin
stretched over wasted bones
so gaunt, so seemingly
devoid of life you knew
he had to rattle if he moved.
my mother had been told
that we must come, and soon,
so here we stood, . . . I
with my brother and my mother,
the three of us all
huddled miserably together
staring down at him.

they took the life sustaining
tent away, and when my father
focussed on my mother's face
this poor exhausted creature
sat up, held out stick arms
and cried an untelligible cry,
his voice the voice of death,
his need the desparate
need of love

sometimes I waken in the night
remembering how I failed.

. . . TO DUST

so many things
to think about and
some of them
are bones.

lank skeletons hang
limp in cold, stale air,
a skull, once proudly worn
by wolf, or fox
or bear, bleached
beauty now, an ornament
upon a wall, a whiteness
for the sun to play upon.
small heaps of woodland
creatures bones, half
buried in damp, leafy
mold, long since abandoned
by an owl and left
for ants to prowl about.
no bones at all
for shrimp or crab
and still they hang together,
those exoskeletal crustaceans.

and finally white
powdery dust blows
through the canyons, whirling
before the wind and once again
the wheel has turned and
reaches for the sun.

NO RETURN

two sweaters
still I feel
the cold

the cold is
in my heart
like brittle

icy splinters
piercing to
its deepest part

I long for spring
again to run
beside a stream

to follow
spinning leaves
in rushing flow

to watch kingfishers
swooping low
and scooping up

their prey
then flying off
to feed their young

my young
have grown
now feed their own

the smell of
new-cut grass
still best of all

as ever in
the past
but I

can never in
this life again
be spring

RETURN

it's hard for me
to believe
that spring

has touched me
again . . . I am in love
with spring

and with myself
being spring
touched

the time of
the fullness
of flowering

has come . . .
it's hard for me
to believe

that once again
I shiver
with delight

the sun warms
my body and sparks
fly from my skin

and at night
with stars
exploding

all around
I shiver with
delight . . .

ON READING CHINESE POETRY

this grey October morning
in my green willow chair
I read Chinese poems
by the open window
and feel the fog's chill
drift up the hill.

bright feathered quail
call softly
outside my door.

INDIGO ISLAND

early morning,
the silver sky
feathered with
saffron and rose . . .
in the crawfish ponds
blue herons
and snowy egrets
quietly fishing

ISLA ANIL

al alba
el cielo de plata
plumado de rosa
y azafrán . . .
en las charcas de pez
airones azules
y aigretes níveos
pescando tranquilo . . .

A POEM FOR DREAMERS

how luminous the dreams
on such a night when streams
of stars are poured
across the sky.
on such a night the wild
geese fly to winter lands
flung wide in bands
of beauty winging high.

dawn drops a veil
on misty dreams when she
has brought her frail
and rose-red brush
and swept each star away
to let the sun explode
across the blazing
face of day.

then wild geese disappear in light
are seen no more till dreaming night
has come . . . and stars
once more are poured
across the sky

DREAMING REALITY

I cannot tell if
I am truly happy as
I believe myself to be . . .
there are moments in my
span of time when welling up
inside me comes a sense
of all my senses . . . . . as if
now, in this space, the
secrets are so joyous
there is no room inside
to hold them all.
I feel that I am
standing poised on
thresholds of some other
elements in time . . . another
plane where curling
seagreen waves are me,
the humming songs
of hiving bees are my own
song and every day the rising
sun is poured into a golden bowl of expectations.

no matter if I'm only dreaming . . .
in every way the happiness
seems real . . . and I
can be aware of pure delight

INTO FOREVER

toes opening, closing
clutching wet
sand beneath my feet

an ocean flows
and ebbing . . . opens
up my eyes

wriggling in
the watery sand small
phosphorescent things

vaulted, intensely dark
the sky and bright
the whirling stars

each spinning
down its own
accustomed path

and I am one
with ocean . . . sky . . .
and stars

spinning
down my
own

THE SPECIAL DAY

hateful pigtails, not long enough
to fall with grace, just standing
stark and straight beyond my naked ears.
humiliations to be born with childhood's
blind acceptance, but on this summer day
not even they could mar the bliss I knew
would soon be mine, for we, my friend
and I, hugged tightly to our hearts
a gift, a day to be together
with not a single grown-up
to say what we should do.

shoeless, sockless, we set out,
bare feet itching for a mountain stream,
to slide along its shallow bed,
to climb and cling to slippery rocks
while shrieking cries of pure delight.
the cold clear water sang our song,
the very one we would have sung
had we known how. At times the forest
closed above our heads, and welcoming
the cool, we'd rest a while in shade,
but soon, unable to resist the lure
we'd run to play again in dappled light
and rushing crystal water.

I still remember woodland violets,
shy blossoms barely seen above the musty
mold of centuries. I feel the softness
of the downy moss and see the multihues
of lichens and lacy shadows cast by
stream-side ferns. I drank that day
into myself, letting it fill my deepest
part, and like a vessel overflowing
yet guarding close the precious flow,
I hold the memory within me still.

EARTH'S AURA

invisible, untouchable,
encircling our earth
a ring . . .
evolving consciousness
waiting to be tapped
by us who dwell
upon this planet.
what if we
feel it now
already streaming
through our veins,
already firing
all our senses?

what if this is the force
we seek and sleepwalkers
and quiet mystic dreamers
already are the willing acolytes?

perhaps we sense our future
and know there is no time
to lose . . .

Julia Cunningham

I AM A DRAGON

I am a dragon. Cherish me.
I have no other than my fire for comfort
by scale and claw and fang made solitary.
I hide my dreadsome shape in shadow and in cave
peering out for friend
in my innocence calling to the eagle,
"Come! Dip your wings to me, speak but one word
I do not ask for more." But even he
passes by without the turning of an eye.
Sometimes I walk a forest, scraping sides
pretending that leaves are gentle giant's hands
and I his beast, obedient to his whim,
leashed to his chain, a place beside his hearth.
O hear me, ancient world! Take me back
into the fields of time where I was once
protector of a princess, victim of a prince.
Lance me to the heart, death is less a misery
than what I am.
I am a dragon. Set me free!

TRAIN WHISTLE

I knew them all — the long and lonely calls
that pulled me out of sleep, up by the roots.
On summer nights I lay walled in by prairie grass,
star-burned by the sky, longing to be gone
to follow the high, crescendoed cry
myself a streak of sound, desire so strong
I seemed to rise quick like a bird, a lark,
until I rode astride what I had heard,
a partner to the dark with me above the train
sending my voice across the turning world
again, again, again!

ON RE-ENTERING A HOUSE ALONE

The journey was too far to allow
the continued presence of roses
or the heater left on to warm the abandonment,
dust had come to cover the caring of the table tops
grimed windows dimmed the outer light
greying the wall and all the paintings retreated
losing their lines, haphazard oblongs, blur upon blur.
But this was not the sorrow that closed the throat,
let the suitcase fall forlorn upon the floor.
Why, as once upon a time, why weren't you standing
as I came, standing in the door?

HAVE YOU EVER?

Have you ever travelled in a rug
floating down the river of blue threads
at halt where the reds squared with room for resting
then on through the vertical gates of brown
to the green triangles of lawn as soft as cloud
for rolling on? Have you ever?
Have you ever whirled inside a purple circle
spinning into yellow where the sun shone so clear
you burned off your parlor pallor and became burnt sienna
then cooled within the deep of violet?
Have you ever?
Have you ever truly journeyed in a rug
until, unwelcome, a voice said "Look at her,
dreaming again, staring at nothing!"
and you came back. laughing inside yourself
returned, renewed, the voyage taken
and no one knowing where the wonder was?
Have you ever?

THERE IS NO OTHER WAY

There is no other way to grow
but as the rose,
darkly rooted, exposed
to violence of sky, of blight.
There is no other way to be
but thorned, cut and cutting,
prisoner, free only to stand
as straight as is the stem
or bent, depending on the nourishment,
the difference contained in chance
whether the wind is kind
or the earth salted.
The valor is the flower, faulted or rare,
that parts the air one hour, one day
and in one breath of giving
shall disclose the spirit.
There is no other way
but as the rose.

SOMEWHERE IN FRANCE

Root me under poplars
align me long with these
green spires that tomorrow rise
higher to sky, to star
than ever I.
Let my voice be leaves,
far songs that never sang
from out my lesser fires.
Let anyone who grieves
forget a marking stone,
know me on the wind
that violins the trees
and orchestrates my bones.

INVITATION TO MUSIC

I am within, I have become
I have reached and been found
and all of me sings!
I soar, my wings spread to the theme,
Like wind, the strings of cello, viola
Violin lift me out in circles
wider than earth,
a flute is measure to my breath
I cry, I shout
I am the trumpet and the horn
all mine, all free of anything but sound!

Be! Forget the ground and fly!
Rebirth, reborn
I call to you with love —
Come! Share this sky with me!

AN AUTUMN APPEARANCE OF ANGELS

"Listen to the leaves," they said,
  arrived between the trees cathedral tall
  and fiery as the wood.
"To understand must first be understood
  these falling voices.
  Reach beyond their whispers
  hear the tone, the unison of scarlet, copper, flame,
  as certain music as the oldest stone
  sweet-sculptured to our image.
  Each single leaf, alive or come to dust
  carries our speech
  and as their carmine, tangerine and gold
  falling sings, telling of us, our when and where and why
  then will you hear us speak as we descend the sky
  to fold you, understanding, in our wings."

MIRACLE

I took the journey head-first
down into the far below
and surfaced on the last bubble
holding a rose.

I dug a hole at midnight
by the light of no moon
entrenched the petals one by one
and waited with the owls

One, two, three, a dozen
Up, up, up they came
calling out poems.
Want a song?
Tell me. They're yours.

COYOTE

Did I want recognition
from this creature of immaculate beauty
down from his mountain hideout?
Or was it atavistic kinship
impelling me toward him
as he stood motionless in the olive grove,
balanced like a runner
waiting for the race to start,
ears and nose assessing the danger?
It was the shift of my foot
that lost him.
I felt abandoned
as he vanished.

CROW

You swerve off the telephone pole
making that ungodly racket
hoarse-throated
reiterating impudent nothings
rudely flapping across my garden
ignoring me
signalling your companions
with your raucous caw.

You're a bow-legged misfit
waddling through my field
straight man
on the vaudeville circuit
done up in your dress suit
with the pants cut off too short.

And yet I love you best of all the birds
because you transport me
to the pine trees
behind my Grandmother's house
where I hear you
cawing, cawing.

DEER HUNT

In the morning light I followed your two-pronged hoof prints
incised like chinese characters in the wet earth.
Now it is almost dusk, time you will be watering again
and I walk into the scene timeless as a tapestry.

Here is the hollowed oak, storm split,
still shadowing a freshened stream
angling down the emerald hillside,
oak clumps tufting down its flank.

You are not yet woven into the fabric of this landscape
though there is a scent of your presence here.
In the silence of distant motors humming
I wait, my retina alert to receive your image.

Suddenly you stand on the ridge, tensed against the sky.
My lens eye focused, imprints you on the tapestry,
now complete. Your eyes rivet and follow
as I walk on, around the bend of the road.

VOID I

Motor idles hot
waiting for red to green
corner of my eye
brings the telephone pole
into vision where
a torn poster
hangs listless
headlining last month's
Hot Rock Band.
Breeze sets
poster flapping,
now unread.

Memory flutters through
futility of lost encounters,
dissolves
as green light
sends surge of motors
forward.

VOID II

Snaking through
blaze of autumn heat
the Sicilian road
coils through
an unpeopled landscape to
"Entrata al Lido"
bathers have deserted
the long bath-house row
doors of dirty green
indolent waters
lap the shore
where the newspaper
fades on empty sands
and a broken chair
tilts under the canvas
sagging from its bent frame
rust-encrusted sign flaps
"Drink Ciapazzi - Acqua Minerale."

JUMP-ROPE SONG

Wind chime and flute and buzzing of bees
dried fig-leaf rustle and autumn sneeze
owl-hoot, bird-whistle, and dew-drop fall
broom-sweep and door-slam, telephone call.
Chain-saw rasp and cry-baby cry
hummingbird whir and housewife's sigh
clip-clopping pony, neighing filly
tough-boy shouts and girls' giggle-silly.
Wind in the rigging, flapping sail snap
airplane drone, popping bottle-top cap
hot rock band, political oration
toot of the train at the railway station.

SIDEWALK SONG

Hopscotching over rain pools
trapped in sidewalk depressions,
she leaps over her dream world
floats down
through watery reflections,
clambering through leaf-over-leaf maze
to center world.
Center earth tilts
to reverse,
ends in sky.
She drifts serene on white cloud,
white cloud scatters at jump-off.
Merrily sloshing
she muddies her dream world
scampers back to here.
Toe-kicking, shambling,
she ambles
to waiting grubby desk rows,
smudged papers, stubby pencils
and eraser bits.

GRACKLES

attentive to the morning light
arrange along telephone lines,
quarter notes on a staff
of bird gossip medley.
Wires sway under late arrivals
bony claws tighten to balance,
release to sidle,
quarter notes shift to rearranged melodies
and new pecking orders establish.

COASTAL MORNING

Fog lies silver gray on the land
heavy as mercury
it has the mystery of an El Greco cloud
only cherubs are not there.
Birds are not hungry this morning
the garden quiet, like a closed park.
Mountains are gone, near pines
pencil points on a white paper.
A bulldozer coughs, settles into its daily drone,
but more muffled, less irritating.

I pull on my winter bathrobe, hug myself close,
the coffee is strong and hot.
We gossip about neighbors. The morning radio
blares out its usual traffic-jam frenzy
down in L.A.
Up from the oil platform, sound of the fog-horn
drifts on a fog-sea. With a shift of wind,
though there is no wind up here,
we suddenly don't hear it anymore.
My crow flies across my vision.

JOGGERS

I see them coming down the final mile
with perspiration dripping through their smile
it's almost like a ritual, pagan dance.

The boy, loose-jointed, springing in his stance
the girl, determined in her steady style
I see them coming down the final mile.

With breathing timed in simple elegance
their rhythm has strange power to beguile
it's almost like a ritual, pagan dance.

One look confirms they are not dilettantes
the evenness with which they both advance
I see them coming down the final mile.

Briefly now they run in single file
and break the balanced pattern for awhile
it's almost like a ritual, pagan dance.

Amazed, I watch this strangest tribal trial
that brings about their blissful state of trance
I see them coming down the final mile
it's almost like a ritual, pagan dance.

PICASSO

"Yo El Rey"

I am the black eye of the bull
I am the Minotaur
I aim — for the bull's-eye
hit the mark — each time
eye mark I — in time
intense eye — fierce eye
pierce the flesh — slash
the female to fragments — flatten
forms to cardboard cut-outs
I woo woman
entomb the woman — plane the woman
gape the mouth in anguish
gape the beast's mouth
Guernica —
war against mankind
war against woman
Yo — the man
the King
the Eye

.

ACKNOWLEDGEMENTS

Katy Peake

Hunter's Wife. Published in *Spectrum,* Winter 1971.

Kit Tremaine

Hawk. Published in California State Poetry Society Quarterly, Vol. VII, No. 3. Set to music by Harold Budd and performed in the US, Europe.

No Return. Won poetry award at Santa Barbara Writers Conference June 1981.

On Reading Chinese Poetry. Published in California State Poetry Society Quarterly, Vol. VI, No. 3, Fall, 1979. Set to music by Harold Budd for concert in Santa Barbara, Fall 1980.

A Poem for Dreamers. Set to music by Daniel Lentz under the title *"Point Conception"* and performed in New York, Belgium and France.

Julia Bates

Joggers. Published in California State Poetry Society Quarterly, Winter 1980.

Void I. Published in California State Poetry Society Quarterly, Summer-Fall 1980.

Crow. First prize, 1980 Ventura College Creative Writing Contest.

Coyote. Published in California State Society Quarterly, Spring-Summer 1979 and in *Celebration,* California State Poetry Society, 1980.

*Printed and bound December 1981 in
Santa Barbara by Mackintosh & Young.
Set in Scotch Roman by Aaron Young.
Design by Terri Wright.
50 copies have been handbound,
numbered and signed by the authors.*